21 DAY SELF LOVE CHALLENGE

It's Time to Start Loving Yourself

IVRALINE J. APPLEWHITE

RELENTLESS
PUBLISHING

21 Day Self Love Challenge : It's Time to Start Loving Yourself

Published By :

Relentless Publishing House, LLC

www.relentlesspublishing.com

ISBN: 9781948829427

First Edition: January 2020

10 9 8 7 6 5 4 3 2 1

Selfie NATION

INTRODUCTION

Welcome to the Selfie Nation 21 Day Self Love Challenge beautiful women. You have taken the step to join other beautiful women as yourself that have chosen to operate in the energy of love and positiveness and shed any negative or unproductive energies. It is love that freed you and you must operate in love to feel love. How can love truly enter if you have built walls around your heart due to past pain, disappointments, grief, regrets, unforgiveness, etc. This 21-day challenge is to encourage you to connect with you, my beautiful sister. May your mind be opened and renewed to the point that you continue the path to finding self and the true beauty within. Change is not easy, if it were then everyone would do it quickly. I challenge you to come out of your comfort zone and old mindsets to the newness of the unknown in you and life. During this time and beyond, allow yourself to be as a child exploring its world after learning to walk. You are worth it. I am rooting and praying for you. Now let's have some fun and introspection. Be blessed.

DAY 1

Inspiration of the Day:

I will give thanks to you because I have been so amazingly and miraculously made. Your works are miraculous, and my soul is fully aware of this.

Psalm 139:14 GW

Action:
Take a selfie

Words of Support:

You must see yourself. This selfie is your starting point and your reminder of how far you have come and grown when you look back. If you are not use to taking selfies, it may be uncomfortable at first but in time you'll get the hang of it with practice. One good thing about digital cameras and cell phones of today, if you don't like the photo, you can delete it, and take another.

How do you feel about your self?

_____

_____

_____

_____

_____

_____

_____

_____

_____

_____

_____

_____

_____

_____

_____

_____

I am beautifully flawed

I love everything about me

My selfie ROCKS!

DAY 2

Inspiration of the Day:

"People never care how much you know until they know how much you care."

John C. Maxwell

Action:

Read and write down a quote that inspires you

Words of Support:

Choose a quote or scripture that motivates and/or resonates with you. There are many influential people in the world. If you're unsure of where to start, search quotes of someone you admire. You may find many words of knowledge that inspire you, for the moment just choose one.

Write down your quote.

_____

_____

_____

_____

_____

_____

_____

_____

_____

_____

_____

_____

_____

_____

DAY 3

Inspiration of the Day:

So be careful! "If your brother or sister in God's family does something wrong, warn them. If they are sorry for what they did, forgive them.

Luke 17:3 ERV

Action:
Forgive yourself

Words of Support:

There is a reason you decided to take this challenge. When I began my journey, I was not loving myself to the fullest. No one was responsible for this but me. I had offended myself and as we do others, I needed to apologize. I looked in the mirror, spoke my truth, apologized, cried, and forgave me. From that point on, it was up to me to love Ivraline the way she needed even if others didn't. You are the master of your internal kingdom and control what you allow within. If you have given this power to others for one reason or another, it is time to reclaim your power with notice of under new management.

Write down one thing that you need to forgive yourself from doing or allowed to happen.

DAY 4

Inspiration of the Day:

A smile makes people happy. Good news makes them feel better.

Proverbs 15:30 ERV

Action:

Participate in an enjoyable activity that you've not done in awhile

Words of Support:

Have fun today engaging in an old favorite pastime or hobby. Life get's busy and for one reason or another we can find ourselves forgetting about the things that used to bring us joy. Keep it simple so as not to cause any unnecessary stress; this activity is a refresher not a stressor.

Write down where you are going to go and what you are going to do.

_____

_____

_____

_____

_____

_____

_____

_____

_____

_____

_____

_____

_____

_____

_____

DAY 5

Inspiration of the Day:

"Gratitude is a powerful catalyst for happiness. It's the spark that lights a fire of joy in your soul."

Amy Collette

Action:

Write down 21 things that you are thankful for in your life.

Words of Support:

Use this time to focus on what you have and not what you lack or desire. There are many that don't have what you may be thankful for or take for granted. There is abundance even in your lack. Think about it. Are your basic needs for food, clothing, and shelter being met? Are you healthy or managing your medical conditions? Do you have people to lean on in your time of need? These things may/may not appear small to you but are the answer to someone else's prayers.

Write down 21 things that you are thankful for in your life.

1._____

2._____

3._____

4._____

5._____

6._____

7._____

8._____

9._____

10._____

11._____

12._____

13._____

14._____

15._____

16._____

17._____

18._____

19._____

20._____

21._____

I will not live in unforgiveness

I will be grateful for everything that comes in my life

I will fill myself with positive words!

DAY 6

Inspiration of the Day:

"Music was my refuge. I could crawl into the space between the notes and curl my back to loneliness."

Maya Angelou

Action:

Listen to your favorite hype song

Words of Support:

My thought is that most of us have at least one song that inspires and gives us an instant boost of positive energy. Positive energy is healing energy which changes the world within. Start your day with this song. Keep your spirits up by listening to your song and others that inspire you as many times as needed throughout the day to stay positive. If needed, make a playlist of songs that positively inspire you so you can locate quickly.

What is your favorite hype song?

_____

_____

Why do you like this song?

_____

_____

_____

_____

_____

_____

DAY 7

Inspiration of the Day:

"We need to find God, and he cannot be found in noise and restlessness. God is the friend of silence. See how nature – trees, flowers, grass – grows in silence, see the stars, the moon and the sun, how they move in silence.... We need silence to be able to touch souls."

Mother Teresa

Action:

Pray, meditate, journal, or sit with self ten minutes.

Words of Support:

I believe prayer changes things and helps to maintain inner peace. As we purge ourselves of the stressors and worries of the day and/or life through prayer, meditation, or journaling, it, helps pour out what is within in a positive manner. When under pressure, the energy must go somewhere, some pour out on those they love which can harm relationships at times. Here is an alternative to get it out and preserve you and your relationships. In this time, just

17

let your thoughts and feelings flow. This is your private time so go where you feel you can freely speak, as those you love do not always need to hear what you really think. We are human and not all our thoughts are pure so we must manage ourselves, as there are consequences to all choices. God knows how you feel so your thoughts are no surprise to Him. Being honest with yourself and speaking your truth as you see it at that moment may give relief along with clarity and insight into other perspectives. Feel free to continue this process throughout the challenge and beyond.

What did you discover about yourself?

_____

_____

_____

_____

_____

_____

_____

_____

_____

_____

_____

_____

_____

_____

_____

I will love all of me

I will explore new things

I will be spontaneous

DAY 8

Inspiration of the Day:

"Success is an act of exploration. That means the first thing you have to find is the unknown. Learning is searching; anything else is just waiting."

Dale Dauten

Action:

Explore a new place

Words of Support:

When learning new things, your brain is activated, as you must engage to process the activity in which you seek to accomplish. If there is a place, you have told yourself, I want to go there one day, do it. Enjoy the experience by taking in the environment and learning about this new place. Share with another so you may hear yourself recount the events and experience which stimulates your mind.

What new place will you discover?

_____

_____

Why did you choose this place?

_____

_____

_____

_____

_____

_____

DAY 9

Inspiration of the Day:

We are confident that God listens to us if we ask for anything that has his approval. We know that he listens to our requests. So we know that we already have what we ask him for.

1 John 5:14-15 GW

Action:

Write down answered prayers or requests

Words of Support:

Think on when God answered your prayer. Sometimes we must look back to see how God has kept us no matter what we have encountered to see that if He did it once, He can do it again. Proof that He answered your prayers and you are still alive. Look at your list and give thanks as someone is praying for that which you received an answer.

Write down your answered prayer requests.

_____

_____

_____

_____

_____

_____

_____

_____

_____

_____

_____

_____

_____

_____

DAY 10

Inspiration of the Day:

*"When we love, we always strive to become better than we are.
When we strive to become better than we are, everything around us
becomes better too."*

Paulo Coelho

Action:

Write at least one thing that you are hoping to do or receive.

Words of Support:

*Hope is a motivator as it inspires us to look for what has not been
seen. It keeps you on the path to pursuit. As you pursue, you grow
because you are taking the steps needed to achieve that which you
desire. You may start small or go big, it's up to you.*

Write at least one thing that you are hoping to do or receive.

_____

_____

_____

_____

_____

_____

_____

_____

_____

_____

_____

_____

_____

_____

DAY 11

Inspiration of the Day:

"Colors, like features, follow the changes of the emotions."

Pablo Picasso

Action:

Wear your favorite color and take a selfie

Words of Support:

Congratulations, you have made it halfway through this challenge. Have some fun today by wearing your favorite color and taking a selfie to see your progress. Compare your initial photo and the photo of today. How are you different: is your smile a little brighter, did it take you a little less time to take that selfie, do you feel somewhat better internally, etc.? I am believing that you are already changing for the best. Keep it up overcomer.

What is your favoirte color(s)?

_____

Why is that your favorite color?

_____

_____

_____

How did your feel in your favorite color
taking a selfie?

_____

_____

_____

_____

DAY 12

Inspiration of the Day:

"Peace is the result of retraining your mind to process life as it is, rather than as you think it should be."

Wayne W. Dyer

Action:

Evaluate your relationships and make plans to address any relationship that steals your peace.

Words of Support:

Peace is priceless. Take this time to evaluate your relationships and the people you allow to pour into you. Is the energy positive or negative? Relationships will have ups and downs. Look deeper into the core reason why you are connected to this individual. If you find areas that challenge your peace, it is up to you as to your course of action. For some relationships it may be that it is time to speak up and express yourself. The individual may not recognize how they make you feel and value you enough to be conscientious of their actions during interaction. For others their season may be over and now it is time to say goodbye in love to a relationship that may have once been of benefit to a previous stage in your life. You are in control of you. As such, you get to decide to whom you give access.

Write down your evalutaions of your relationships.

_____

_____

_____

_____

_____

_____

_____

_____

_____

_____

_____

_____

_____

Selfie**NATION**
Declaration

I will no longer allow toxicity
in my life. I will create a
peaceful atmosphere,
maintain and protect it. I
deserve to live without drama.

DAY 13

Inspiration of the Day:

"Food is symbolic of love when words are inadequate."

Alan D. Wolfelt

Action:

Try a new food or restaurant

Words of Support:

Many of us know comfort food is real. Take this day to get out of your comfort zone and try a new dish or go to a restaurant that you've never been. Have fun and be open. It is up to you on how daring or conservative you are today. Just take in the experience. You either find that you enjoyed the dish/ environment or that you're not planning to try it again. Either way, you learned something new about yourself and your likes which is always a plus.

What new food or restaurant did you try?

_____

Why did you make that choice?

_____

_____

_____

Describe your experience.

_____

_____

_____

_____

_____

_____

DAY 14

Inspiration of the Day:

"Once you replace negative thoughts with positive ones, you'll start having positive results."

Willie Nelson

Action:

Write down 21 positive things about yourself.

Words of Support:

Positiveness just as negativity is a mindset that has been established through habit. Declare that today you break the shackle of negativity and will seek to view yourself and life through a more positive lens. This will not happen overnight and takes practice. As you face your day, attempt to manage your thoughts by processing your feeling and evaluating the situation through many perspectives. For example, if someone states something that you find offensive, stop and attempt to evaluate what was the individual trying to express. Not everyone is an expert at communicating so it could be that what was meant to be said came out wrong. You cannot control them, but you can control how you respond. Respond positively to negativity. It takes two to argue and if you don't engage there's nothing to discuss. I know this is easier said than done as I had to practice myself on my journey.

Write down 21 things that you like about yourself.

1._____

2._____

3._____

4._____

5._____

6._____

7._____

8._____

9._____

10._____

11._____

12._____

13._____

14._____

15._____

16._____

17._____

18._____

19._____

20._____

21._____

I will add value to my relationships and make sure they add value to me. I will not keep anyone around me that sucks the life out of me.

DAY 15

Inspiration of the Day:

"A dream doesn't become reality through magic; it takes sweat, determination and hard work."

Colin Powell

Action:

Write down your goals for the next three years

Words of Support:

What are you willing to pursue? Your dreams cannot manifest in your life without you. You have the power to make your dreams come true as it is your belief in yourself and not in others that brings what you desire to pass. Open yourself up to possibilities that are beyond what you can see and believe in yourself. You have everything that you need to live your life inside of you, sometimes it just needs to be activated.

Write down your goals for the next three years.

_____

_____

_____

_____

_____

_____

_____

_____

_____

_____

_____

_____

_____

_____

DAY 16

Inspiration of the Day:

"Self-preservation is the first law of nature."

Samuel Butler

Action:

Pamper yourself

Words of Support:

You must take care of yourself to have the energy to take care of others. You cannot add to others if you are depleted. Time for an energy fill up. Take this day to do something for you however small. What's insignificant to another may be of great value to you.

How did you pamper yourself?

_____

_____

_____

Why did you choose this form of pampering?

_____

_____

_____

Describe your experience.

_____

_____

_____

DAY 17

Inspiration of the Day:

"Carry out a random act of kindness, with no expectation of reward, safe in the knowledge that one day someone might do the same for you."

Princess Diana

Action:

Do a random act of kindness

Words of Support:

Helping others blesses you and feeds your spirit positively. The reward that you receive within yourself for being a blessing to another I hope will inspire you to identify other opportunities where you can be of assistance. Whether you're volunteering at an event or just identifying a random person in the community that you can bless, you have now become the answer to someone's prayers by using your gifts and/or resources.

What random act of kindness did you do?

_____

_____

_____

Why did you choose do this random act
of kindess?

_____

_____

_____

How did it make you feel?

_____

_____

_____

DAY 18

Inspiration of the Day:

"Exercise not only changes your body, it changes your mind, your attitude, and your mood."

Unknown Author

Action:

Participate in a physical activity

Words of Support:

Time to move that beautiful body today. Increased activity is a benefit to your overall health. Exerting energy, increases energy, as it builds your capacity and/or tolerance over time. Think about it, you may be able to do more/ less today than you once did. What happened? Your capacity either increased or decreased for one reason or another. Either way, it does not matter as you are moving forward and increasing your capacity as of your current state. Focus on moving more today whether that is taking a walk, participating in an exercise class, or going to the gym. Greater for you is not greater for another. Have fun.

What physical activity did you choose?

_____

_____

Why did you choose do this physical activity?

_____

_____

_____

Will you do it again? Why or why not?

_____

_____

_____

DAY 19

Inspiration of the Day:

"Since you get more joy out of giving joy to others, you should put a good deal of thought into the happiness that you are able to give."

Eleanor Roosevelt

Action:

Meet a friend for lunch, coffee, tea or dinner.

Words of Support:

We are social creatures by design so you cannot get away from this fact. Time to get out and have some fun with another. You choose the activity; enjoy yourself and stay positive. You must make time to connect.

Whom did you meet?

_____

Where did you meet?

_____

_____

How was the exeperience?

_____

_____

_____

Will you make this a regular activity?
Why or why not?

_____

_____

DAY 20

Inspiration of the Day:

"Encourage, lift and strengthen one another. For the positive energy spread to one will be felt by us all. For we are connected, one and all."

Deborah Day

Action:

Encourage another person

Words of Support:

We all need to be encouraged, as life can get hard even if you are not in pursuit of change now. Take time today to encourage another whether it be your spouse, child, family, friend, partner or a stranger. It does not matter who you pour into today, just share your positive energy.

Whom did you choose to encourage?

_____

_____

How did you encourage them?

_____

_____

_____

How did it make you feel to brighten
someone's day?

_____

_____

_____

DAY 21

Inspiration of the Day:

"If you can't fly then run, if you can't run then walk, if you can't walk then crawl, but whatever you do you have to keep moving forward."

Dr. Martin Luther King Jr.

Action:

Take a selfie!

Words of Support:

Congratulations on completing this 21 Day Self Love Challenge! You have committed to loving you which is always of benefit. May you continue to challenge yourself to grow, heal, and live a healthy and fulling life filled with love, joy, peace, good health, forgiveness, kindness, and prosperity. Your light has been turned on and now it is up to you to keep it shining bright by feeding it good things. In the words of Paulo Coelho "Jesus lived a life that was full of joy and contradictions and fights, you know? If they were to paint a picture of Jesus without contradictions, the gospels would be fake, but the contradictions are a sign of authenticity." Continue to live life in your authenticity and love your amazing self. Be blessed.

I will not put an uneccessary pressure on myself to be perfect or a superwoman. I will respect my self and and treat myself like the Queen I am.

ABOUT THE AUTHOR

I vraline J. Applewhite is a God-fearing woman whose professional work experience has been in social services. She is an inspirational author, has an MBA, loves ladybugs, is humorous, and strives to see the silver lining in life experiences.